ACTS 13–28

Part 2: God's Power at the Ends of the Earth

12 STUDIES FOR INDIVIDUALS OR GROUPS

LifeGuide®
BIBLE STUDIES

PHYLLIS J. LE PEAU

ivp

An imprint of InterVarsity Press
Downers Grove, Illinois

InterVarsity Press
P.O. Box 1400, Downers Grove, IL 60515-1426
ivpress.com
email@ivpress.com

InterVarsity Press® is the book-publishing division of InterVarsity Christian Fellowship/USA®, a movement of students and faculty active on campus at hundreds of universities, colleges and schools of nursing in the United States of America, and a member movement of the International Fellowship of Evangelical Students. For information about local and regional activities, visit intervarsity.org.

LifeGuide® is a registered trademark of InterVarsity Christian Fellowship.

All Scripture quotations, unless otherwise indicated, are taken from the Holy Bible, New International Version®. NIV®. Copyright ©1973, 1978, 1984 by International Bible Society. Used by permission of Zondervan Publishing House. All rights reserved.

Cover design: Cindy Kiple
Interior design: Jeanna Wiggins
Cover image: volcano eruption: © AZ68 / iStockphoto

ISBN 978-0-8308-3120-3 (print)
ISBN 978-0-8308-6209-2 (digital)

Printed in the United States of America ∞

As a member of the Green Press Initiative, InterVarsity Press is committed to protecting the environment and to the responsible use of natural resources. To learn more, visit greenpressinitiative.org.

P	18	17	16	15	14	13	12	11	10	9	8	7	6	5	4	3	2	1
Y	33	32	31	30	29	28	27	26	25	24	23	22	21	20	19

CONTENTS

GETTING THE
MOST OUT OF
ACTS 13–28

J ust before Acts begins, the disciples are wallowing in the mire of their craven fear, self-doubt and personal shame. Apart from their master, they are a pathetic group indeed (John 20:19; Luke 24:11). However, by the second chapter of Acts, the same men who abandoned Jesus at Gethsemane have become irrepressible dynamos, preaching with utter conviction—and at great personal risk—"the mighty acts of God."

Acts is an important book for us today because it confirms that the power of the Holy Spirit, which transformed the disciples' lives, is the same power that can transform our lives today!

There are many benefits to studying Acts:

- *Acts serves as a distant mirror.* We see the dynamics of the earliest church, the nature of their fellowship, the intensity of their prayer life and their out-and-out zeal to declare the saving gospel of Jesus Christ. Our own situation will be called into question. What does it mean to be the church today?

- *Acts emphasizes the primary task of the church—evangelization.* In Acts we see the entire process of calling, healing, empowering and sending people forth to love and obey Jesus Christ.

- *Acts calls us to a vital experience with the Holy Spirit.* The book of Acts reveals the Holy Spirit as the driving force behind all meaningful ministry in Jesus' name.

- *Acts forges a new sense of identity.* The disciples gradually realized they were no longer Jews (at least from the confessional and ceremonial points of view). They slowly began to understand that they were part of that new community of the Spirit that was prophesied in the Hebrew Scriptures. And they saw the need to call all people—Jews and Gentiles—to repentance and fellowship with this new community, the church.

Through these studies by Phyllis J. Le Peau, the explosive power of this living document will touch you. As you work through these studies, may you experience the calling, healing, empowering and sending dynamic of the Holy Spirit.

Louis Quetel

SUGGESTIONS FOR INDIVIDUAL STUDY

1. As you begin each study, pray that God will speak to you through his Word.

2. Read the introduction to the study and respond to the personal reflection question or exercise. This is designed to help you focus on God and on the theme of the study.

3. Each study deals with a particular passage—so that you can delve into the author's meaning in that context. Read and reread the passage to be studied. The questions are written using the language of the New International Version, so you may wish to use that version of the Bible. The New Revised Standard Version is also recommended.

4. This is an inductive Bible study, designed to help you discover for yourself what Scripture is saying. The study includes three types of questions. *Observation* questions ask about the basic facts: who, what, when, where and how. *Interpretation* questions delve into the meaning of the passage. *Application* questions help you discover the implications of the text for growing in Christ. These three keys unlock the treasures of Scripture.

Write your answers to the questions in the spaces provided or in a personal journal. Writing can bring clarity and deeper understanding of yourself and of God's Word.

5. It might be good to have a Bible dictionary handy. Use it to look up any unfamiliar words, names or places.

6. Use the prayer suggestion to guide you in thanking God for what you have learned and to pray about the applications that have come to mind.

7. You may want to go on to the suggestion under "Now or Later," or you may want to use that idea for your next study.

SUGGESTIONS FOR MEMBERS OF A GROUP STUDY

1. Come to the study prepared. Follow the suggestions for individual study mentioned above. You will find that careful preparation will greatly enrich your time spent in group discussion.

2. Be willing to participate in the discussion. The leader of your group will not be lecturing. Instead, he or she will be encouraging the members of the group to discuss what they have learned. The leader will be asking the questions that are found in this guide.

3. Stick to the topic being discussed. Your answers should be based on the verses which are the focus of the discussion and not on outside authorities such as commentaries or speakers. These studies focus on a particular passage of Scripture. Only rarely should you refer to other portions of the Bible. This allows for everyone to participate in in-depth study on equal ground.

4. Be sensitive to the other members of the group. Listen attentively when they describe what they have learned. You may be surprised by their insights! Each question assumes a variety of answers. Many questions do not have "right" answers, particularly questions that aim at meaning or application. Instead the questions push us to explore the passage more thoroughly.

When possible, link what you say to the comments of others. Also, be affirming whenever you can. This will encourage some of the more hesitant members of the group to participate.

5. Be careful not to dominate the discussion. We are sometimes so eager to express our thoughts that we leave too little opportunity for others to respond. By all means participate! But allow others to also.

6. Expect God to teach you through the passage being discussed and through the other members of the group. Pray that you will have an enjoyable and profitable time together, but also that as a result of the study you will find ways that you can take action individually and/or as a group.

7. Remember that anything said in the group is considered confidential and should not be discussed outside the group unless specific permission is given to do so.

8. If you are the group leader, you will find additional suggestions at the back of the guide.

ONE

THE CHARACTER OF EVANGELISM

Acts 13–14

I love evangelism, but I do not consider myself to be a "proclamation evangelist" who speaks the gospel to large groups. I love to lead small group investigative Bible discussions with people who are not believers. In fact I have been known to say, tongue-in-cheek, this is the only way that one can become a Christian. However, I was recently called upon to give a talk to a group of students who were, mostly, not yet Christians.

Just before leaving for campus that day, I spoke to a colleague on the phone. I said, "Pray for me. I am not giving a talk. I am going to preach." The Holy Spirit gave me clarity and passion as I spoke about what it meant to be reconciled to God—to have your soul bought for God. Students responded by wanting to know more about Jesus.

The character of evangelism changed for me that day.

Group Discussion. Think of someone you know who effectively shares the gospel. What qualities do you see in that person?

Personal Reflection. What characteristics and qualities do you have that make sharing the gospel natural for you? What makes it difficult for you to share your faith?

Peter has disappeared, and Luke is ushering Paul to center stage. Peter, the apostle to the Jews, has played his part well and prepared the way for Paul, the apostle to the Gentiles. In this study we will look at Paul's first missionary journey, the beginning of his master plan of evangelism. We will also consider the personal qualities that made Paul effective in the task of evangelism. *Read Acts 13–14.*

1. As you look over these two chapters what qualities do you see in Paul and in Barnabas that made them effective in their ministry?

2. Which of these qualities do you want God to develop in you to make you more effective in communicating the gospel?

3. What role did the church of Antioch play in Paul's first missionary journey (13:1-3; 14:26-28)?

4. In missionary outreach, how do churches today compare and contrast with those of Antioch?

5. Review Paul's message in the synagogue in Pisidian Antioch (13:16-41). What truths of the gospel are communicated?

6. How does Paul's message show sensitivity to his audience and the context?

7. In what relationships and situations do you need this same sensitivity?

8. List the different responses to the gospel (13:7-8, 13, 42-45, 48, 52; 14:1-5) that you see throughout this passage.

9. How did Paul respond to those who rejected the gospel (13:9-11, 46, 51)?

to those who believed (14:9-10, 21-23)?

10. In this passage the response to the gospel by the disciples was to be filled with "joy and the Holy Spirit" (13:52). How prevalent is this in the life of our church today? Explain.

11. People today are not apt to offer sacrifices to those who bring the good news of Jesus. However, in what ways are we faced with the temptation to be "god" in another's life or to take credit for what God has done?

12. Based on how Paul and Barnabas responded to being seen as "gods," how can we respond when this happens to us or when we are tempted to take credit for what God has done?

 Pray about ways that God may want you to grow as a communicator of his good news.

NOW OR LATER

Write a psalm about God based on Acts 14:14-18. Let your heart and mind be free to be creative. Don't be limited to the thoughts in this passage.

TWO

CONFLICT IN THE CHURCH

Acts 15

I n most areas of life, I think I am pretty realistic. When it comes to conflict among believers, however, I tend to be an idealist. I believe that unity is something that God requires of us. Believers should be able to talk, pray and work through conflict—just the way it was worked through by the church in Jerusalem.

However, I am becoming a little more realistic about this. I have experienced several situations in which I felt like I did everything within my power to bring about reconciliation—but failed. The late Kenneth Strachan of the Latin America Mission said, "We all need to live and serve in the constant recognition of our own humanity."

Group Discussion. What are you like when you are in strong disagreement with others?

Personal Reflection. Think about those with whom you are in conflict. Talk to God about it, and let his peace and compassion wash over you as he teaches you.

In this study we will consider ways of handling conflict within the Christian community. *Read Acts 15:1-35.*

1. Describe the conflict that arises between believers in this passage.

2. Describe the steps that were taken to resolve this conflict and the spirit of those involved.

3. What were the results?

4. What principles do you observe that are vital to follow as we face conflict with others in our Christian community?

5. Which of these principles do you struggle the most to implement?

6. *Read Acts 15:36-41.* In what ways do you see (or assume based on the first part of this chapter) unity between Paul and Barnabas?

7. What was the cause of their conflict?

8. Paul and Barnabas decided to agree to disagree and went their separate ways. What were the benefits of this temporary solution?

9. Both Paul and Barnabas seemed to have strong cases for their points of view. Under what kinds of circumstances should we surrender deep convictions when they are challenged by another?

10. No matter how strongly we feel about an issue, we do not see the whole picture. How should that fact affect the way we respond to people with whom we are in conflict?

11. When you are in conflict with others, how does your response compare or contrast with that of Paul and Barnabas?

with the leaders of the church (vv. 1-35)?

Ask God to give you discernment as you face conflict in both the church and your personal life.

NOW OR LATER

Choose one or two of the most significant conflicts in your life. Write out the details of that conflict—cause, how it began, the issues at stake— as clearly as you can see them and what you would like to do for resolution. Now make a list of the principles that you see as you observe the church leaders in conflict. How can these principles be applied to your situation?

THREE

WHAT MUST I DO?

Acts 16

The memory is still vivid. The event was InterVarsity's Urbana Missions Convention. The place, a dormitory room. The person, a young lady from the Bible study group I led.

I sensed the prompting of the Holy Spirit to stop by Susan's room. As I walked in to say hi, she looked up from the booklet she was reading and said, "I would like to become a Christian. Will you help me?"

Group Discussion. What makes it easy for you to obey God? What makes you hesitate?

Personal Reflection. Think back to when you uttered the words, "What must I do to be saved?" either to a friend or to God himself. Praise God for creating a desire for himself in you, and thank him for giving his precious salvation to you.

This dormitory setting was not quite as dramatic as the Philippian jail. But it was just as exciting for me to hear Susan's words as it was for Paul and Silas to hear the jailer's cry, "Sirs, what must I do to be saved?" *Read Acts 16.*

| 1. How do you see Paul directed by God throughout this passage?

| 2. What principles of guidance do you see?

3. When have you experienced God's leading in your life?

4. Paul responded immediately to God's call to preach the gospel in Macedonia. How was his obedience confirmed on arriving in Macedonia?

5. There are many reasons that people reject the gospel. The owners of the slave girl resisted the gospel because of material gain. What are reasons that you see today for rejecting the truth?

6. The slave owners had Paul and Silas jailed. Their response to being beaten and put in jail was to pray and sing hymns. Describe the events of the night that led up to the jailer's question, "What must I do to be saved?" (vv. 23-30).

7. How does your response to opposition and suffering for the gospel compare and contrast to that of Paul and Silas (v. 25)?

8. Paul and Silas speak the truth of the gospel as well as live it out. How do you give both a verbal and a living witness to Jesus?

9. It is clear in the book of Acts that God is concerned that the nations and the world be reached with the gospel. But he is also concerned about reaching individuals. What individuals were affected by Paul's obedience to God's leading (vv. 14, 18, 30-31)? How?

10. What might have been the consequences if Paul had ignored God's call to Macedonia?

11. What person or task might God be calling you to?

What steps do you need to take for immediate and unreserved obedience?

 Ask God to give you courage as you step out in faith to obey him and tell those around you about the good news of the gospel.

NOW OR LATER

Journal about how you obey God. What struggles do you have? When is it most likely that you instantly obey, and when is it more difficult? What consequences have you experienced from not obeying? from obeying? What do you feel about your relationship with God when you obey him? when you don't?

FOUR

AN UNKNOWN GOD

Acts 17

Only a few short decades ago, Christians in the West could assume that most people they met belonged to a church or at least based their lives on Judeo-Christian values. Today, Christians in the West face what Christians in the East have had to cope with for centuries—a wide variety of religious beliefs and practices that often have little in common with Christianity. Paul left us a helpful model of how to cope with a world that cares so little about the truth when he visited the world center of pagan philosophy and religion—Athens.

Group Discussion. What kinds of philosophies do you encounter as you attempt to communicate the gospel in our modern world?

Personal Reflection. Do you feel overwhelmed by the dismal spiritual conditions of this world? Remember and even savor the knowledge that Jesus is Lord over it all—the sin, deceit and pain around us are all subject to his will.

In this passage we will observe how Paul responds to different cultures when he communicated the gospel. *Read Acts 17.*

1. Paul interacts with three cities and three different cultures. Compare and contrast Paul's ministry in Thessalonica and Berea. (What approach did he take? How was his message received by the people? What kinds of results did he have?)

2. In Thessalonica and Berea, as in most places, Paul makes his contacts in the synagogues and speaks almost exclusively from Scripture. When have you seen people come to Christ as a result of looking at Scripture?

3. Describe Paul's approach in Athens.

4. What are the main points of his lecture?

5. How do the people of Athens respond to his teaching?

6. Paul speaks of "the objects of your worship." What are some of the objects of worship for people in our culture?

7. How does the message of Christ speak to these objects of worship?

8. In Athens Paul begins to tell them about the living God with an inscription from one of their altars—"TO AN UNKNOWN GOD." What are "points of truth" from which you can start to communicate the gospel to those in your world?

9. Paul's different approaches show his understanding of culture and his willingness to communicate with people where they are. What are the different groups or cultures that you interact with?

10. Though Paul approaches people differently, the content of his messages are very consistent. Identify this content (vv. 3, 18, 24-28, 30-31).

11. What are ways that you might be tempted to compromise the message of the gospel as you communicate it to certain people?

12. What do you need to do and know in order to more effectively communicate the good news about Jesus to people in your life from different cultures?

Ask the Lord to show you what you have in common with the non-Christians in your life. Pray that you will effectively communicate the gospel to them.

NOW OR LATER

Look more closely at Paul's message to the people in Athens. Write down each example of where he connected with the culture. After the example write the points of truth that he made from each connection. Finally, think of one person with whom you would like to share the gospel. Write down how you might connect with them based on their culture and interests. Then write the points of truth that you might share based on the connection.

FIVE

COMPANIONS IN MINISTRY

Acts 18

J**ust recently,** I visited my childhood pastor and his wife. As I left them, my heart was full of gratitude—gratitude not only for the Wrights but also for the others past and present who have prepared me for outreach. I am thankful for those who have prayed for me, been my friends, walked along with me, listened to me, loved me, encouraged me, corrected me, and cared about my walk with God and my service to others. I enjoy thinking about the people who have touched my life and who have been companions in ministry.

Group Discussion. When have you felt alone in the ministry of bringing others to Christ, and why do you think you felt that way?

Personal Reflection. Close your eyes and think about one person who has profoundly affected your life. What are the ways that this person influenced you?

In this study we will look at some of Paul's companions in ministry and be reminded of the strategic role that relationships with others play in our efforts to evangelize. *Read Acts 18.*

1. List the people in Paul's life that you see in this passage.

2. Let's look more closely at some of these relationships. What was the significance of his relationship with Priscilla and Aquila (vv. 2-4, 18-19)?

3. We are told in 1 Thessalonians 3 and Philippians 4 that Silas and Timothy brought Paul not only good news about the faith and steadfastness of the Thessalonians but also a gift of money from the Philippians. This gift relieved him from having to support himself by leather working. What impact did their relationship have on Paul's life and ministry?

4. When have you been sustained by someone bringing you good news of God's work elsewhere, entering into your ministry, sharing themselves or their home with you, or supporting you financially or in other ways?

5. What keeps you from allowing others to enter into your life and ministry in such ways?

6. Contrast the response of the Jews in Corinth (vv. 4-6) to that of Crispus and his household (vv. 7-8).

7. What message did the Lord speak to Paul in a vision (vv. 9-10)?

8. How was his ministry affected by God's words (v. 11)?

9. In verses 18-23, what do you learn about Paul's relationships?

10. Describe Apollos (vv. 24-26).

11. How was Apollos's ministry affected by his relationship with Aquila and Priscilla (vv. 27-28)?

12. As you review this passage, how do you need to develop, build and nurture relationships that will contribute to your spiritual growth and outreach?

 Thank God for his good gift to you of companions in ministry and for their presence in your life.

NOW OR LATER

Think of several people who have influenced your walk with God. Write each a note of appreciation and tell them specifically how God has used them in your life.

SIX

IN THE NAME
OF JESUS

Acts 19:1–20:12

S ome have described the "Cane Ridge Revival" as the greatest out-
pouring of the power of the Holy Spirit since Pentecost. In August
1801, in western Kentucky, the crowd of ten to twenty-five thousand
began to gather. Sectarian distinctions were forgotten as the Word of
God was preached and the story of redemption was told. Within the
crowd all manner of excitement and expectation broke out. After six or
seven days, the course of Protestantism was changed forever. Churches
were revitalized and thousands of people became Christians.

Group Discussion. How would you like to see the power of God revealed in your Christian community?

Personal Reflection. Often we feel that reading the Bible is our time to
give to God. But he dearly wants to come to us as we study Scripture
and pray. Lay aside your effort right now and commit yourself to ac-
cepting God's grace as you study the Word.

We left Paul in chapter 18 traveling throughout Galatia and Phrygia
"strengthening all the disciples." In this chapter he returns to Ephesus,
where he settles for two and a half years. Great work is done there
during this time, and it radiates out to other cities in the province of
Asia. Luke vividly portrays the effect of Paul's ministry in just a few
scenes in this chapter. *Read Acts 19:1–20:12.*

1. Scan the passage and describe the incidences where you see God's power revealed.

2. Wherever the gospel is communicated with effectiveness there will be both positive and negative responses. What are the positive results throughout this passage?

What are the negative responses?

3. What modern day negative and positive responses have you seen as a result of the gospel being communicated with power?

4. In 19:1-7 Paul encounters some disciples. What is his concern for them?

What did he do to interact with them effectively?

5. What do you see in Paul's relationship with the disciples that might help you in relating to young Christians or your non-Christian friends?

6. Throughout this entire passage it is evident that Paul has a strategy for communicating the gospel. Specifically, what strategy does Paul have for his ministry in Ephesus (19:8-10)?

7. What kind of plan for communicating the gospel would be helpful in your world?

8. What happened with the Jews who were driving out evil spirits in the name of Jesus (19:11-14)? Why?

9. How did this become a testimony to the power of God (19:15-20)?

10. What is the cause of the riot in Ephesus, and how was it settled (19:23-41)?

11. Paul continued to travel and encourage believers as he preached the gospel. What effect did the episode in 20:7-12 have on the crowd?

12. How are you seeing the power of the gospel demonstrated in your own life?

13. How can you prepare yourself for both positive and negative responses as you communicate the gospel of Christ?

 Thank God for the amazing fact that he uses us, sinful human beings, to spread the gospel and advance his kingdom. Thank him for using you.

NOW OR LATER

Think about two or three people with whom you would like to share the gospel. Find a prayer partner, if you do not have one, and pray for your not-yet-Christian friends regularly. Ask God to give you a plan for each person, including such things as getting to know them better, serving and loving them, discovering what their interests are and how to spend time with them, inviting them to look at Jesus' life with you in Scripture and so on. Listen to God and then write down a plan. Prayerfully follow the plan.

SEVEN

SAYING GOODBYE

Acts 20:13-38

I **will see you in heaven."** I nodded, gave him a hug and a kiss, and walked away from his bedside. When I left the room, I wept.

Although it was over twenty-five years ago that I said goodbye to Pop Z, the memory is still deep in my heart.

Group Discussion. Imagine what it would be like to say goodbye to someone when you knew that you would not see them again. Describe your thoughts and feelings.

Personal Reflection. Is the busyness of the world around you crowding you as you seek the face of God? Thank God that he has given you the grace that has brought you to his Word right now, and ask him to still your restless heart as he comes to sit with you. *Read Acts 20:13-38.*

1. What do you see and feel as you read through this passage?

2. What does Paul say about his ministry to the Ephesians (vv. 18-21, 26-27, 31, 33-35)?

3. Which of these do you want to be able to say at the end of your own life? Why?

| 4. What steps do you need to take now in order to be able to do so?

| 5. What are Paul's priorities (vv. 22-25)?

| 6. How do your priorities compare and contrast with his?

| 7. What instructions did Paul give to the leaders of the church at Ephesus (vv. 28-31)?

| 8. According to verse 32, why can Paul leave them with confidence?

9. In summary, according to this passage, why would Paul be able to say with integrity and humility to these leaders, "Follow my example"?

10. Who is in your spiritual care?

11. How are you preparing those that you nurture spiritually to be left with this same confidence?

 Ask God for the courage to say these most important words to those you love and who are under your care.

NOW OR LATER

What would you want to say to those in your spiritual care if you knew that you were going to die? Take time to express your hope, your love, your priorities and your passions for them. Remind them how important it is for God and his Word to be the center of their lives.

EIGHT

FACING OPPOSITION

Acts 21:1–22:21

F ive young men sang

> We rest on Thee—our Shield and our Defender!
> We go not forth alone against the foe;
> Strong in Thy strength, safe in Thy keeping tender,
> We rest on Thee and in Thy name we go.
>
> We rest on Thee our Shield and our Defender!
> Thine is the battle, Thine shall be the praise
> When passing through the gates of pearly splendor,
> Victors—we rest with Thee, through endless days.

as they went to their death, taking the gospel of Jesus Christ to the Auca Indians. Like Paul, they knew that death was a very real possibility. They did not turn aside from what they knew God wanted them to do.

Group Discussion. When have you been warned that something you were about to do could be dangerous? How did you feel? What did you do?

Personal Reflection. What fears do you have about your relationship with Jesus?

In this study we will look at the single-mindedness of Paul in his obedience to God. *Read Acts 21:1-26.*

1. What were the warnings to Paul concerning going to Jerusalem and his response to them (vv. 4-5, 10-13)?

2. How were those who observed Paul affected by his single-mindedness (vv. 14-15)?

3. Think of a person you know who is focused on radical obedience to God. How are you affected by his or her obedience?

4. Paul arrives in Jerusalem, is greeted by the elders and reports what God has done through his ministry. What are the elders concerned about for Paul (vv. 20-25)?

5. How does Paul demonstrate his desire to be at one with the Jewish Christians (v. 26)?

6. *Read Acts 21:27–22:21.* Note how Paul was treated with mob hysteria, assumption and false evidence (21:27-36, 38). What would this have been like for you if you were Paul?

7. How does he respond to all of this (21:37–22:21)?

8. Let's look more closely at his defense. What is the significance of his addressing the listeners as "brothers and fathers"?

9. What other qualities do you see in this defense?

10. How do you usually respond when you find yourself in conflict because of obedience to God?

11. In what ways has this passage motivated you to become more single-minded in your obedience to God's will?

12. What steps do you need to take to become a more obedient disciple of Jesus?

 Tell God of your desire to be obedient. Talk to him about the difficulties that you face because of your sin. Ask him to cleanse you and to help you run the race with fervor.

NOW OR LATER

Take the time to read one or two biographies of men and women who have given their lives for the gospel or who have followed the Lord in radical obedience.

NINE

GOD AT WORK

Acts 22:22–23:35

B eing under God's protection is not a guarantee of physical safety. Being under his protection does guarantee that our Father is with us, has purpose for us and that nothing will happen to us that does not come through his hands. We can live with confidence that our lives on earth will not end until those purposes for us are complete, and ultimately we will end up safe and secure in heaven.

Group Discussion. What are ways that you've seen God work in someone's life?

Personal Reflection. The protection of the Father's strong arms is always around us. Thank him for his mighty but unseen acts that keep you safe and secure as you walk through this life. Praise him for the ultimate safety of heaven.

Paul was so sure of God's hand in his life that he continued to move out boldly with the message of Jesus Christ in spite of intense physical danger. In this passage we will observe God's hand in the life of Paul. *Read Acts 22:22–23:35.*

1. Trace the events in Paul's life as though you were reporting for a newspaper.

2. How do you respond to what you see of Paul here?

3. In Acts 22:22-29, what is the source of the conflict?

4. In 23:1-10, what is the source of the conflict?

How is Paul protected this time?

5. Why was Paul struck on the mouth for saying, "My brothers, I have fulfilled my duty to God in all good conscience to this day" (23:1)? What was he claiming about himself?

6. What would you say is your purpose in life?

7. In Acts 23:12-25 the Jews are frustrated because they cannot get rid of Paul through the law, so they decide to ambush and kill him on their own. How is Paul protected?

8. We have observed God's protection of Paul. How do we see God's care for Paul in a more direct, personal and supernatural way in 23:11?

9. Think about God's hand in your life and ministry. How have you seen him work to protect and direct you toward his will?

10. What do you learn about Claudius Lysias in Acts 23:23-30?

11. How does Claudius Lysias present a picture of our own human nature?

12. In what ways do you need to grow in humbly acknowledging God's hand in your life?

13. How has your hope for God's will to be done in you been affected by looking at God's hand in Paul's life?

 Ask God to show you his active hand in your life.

NOW OR LATER

Spend time journaling about your relationship to God and his hand in your life. Include such things as how he brought you to himself, how he communicates his will for your life to you, when you have resisted that will, the circumstances or things that tend to make you walk away from him or his will, and where you have specifically seen his faithfulness to you.

TEN

FALSELY ACCUSED

Acts 24:1–25:12

O ur dear friend George was falsely accused and tried for heresy.
My husband prayed fervently that God would shut the mouths
of George's accusers and bind their efforts, and that truth would prevail
and bring freedom. He asked God to confound their actions so that their
words would bring out the truth and show up their false accusations.

God chose to do what my husband asked for . . . and George was
exonerated in a dramatic fashion. The words of the accusers brought
condemnation on them. The defense did not even have to present
their case.

The pain, however, in being falsely accused is great. And the damage
is not easily repaired. But George's consistent godly response was an
example to me.

Group Discussion. How do you usually respond when you are falsely
accused?

Personal Reflection. How do you respond to the unfairness in the
world around you? the unfairness in your own life?

In this study we will see how Paul responded to false accusations.
Read Acts 24.

1. What are the accusations brought against Paul by the Jews?

2. What does the extent of the flattery lavished on Felix tell you
about the accusers?

3. How would you describe Paul's defense? (Consider the content and the attitude and tone.)

4. What do you think might be the significance of the fact that Felix was well acquainted with the Way (v. 22)?

5. Why do you think Felix responded to the gospel as he did?

6. When have you known someone to respond to the proclamation of the gospel as Felix did?

What might this mean?

7. *Read Acts 25:1-12.* Two years have passed since his trial, and Festus has become the new governor. The Jews have not given up. They continue to plot to kill Paul and ask Festus to have him transferred to Jerusalem. Festus refuses and tells the Jewish leaders to come to Caesarea for the trial. What evidence is there in this passage that Festus knows Paul is innocent?

8. Describe a time you have been falsely accused because of your faith.

9. Why does Festus suggest that Paul go back to Jerusalem to be on trial?

How does Paul respond to this idea?

10. What do you think of Paul's response?

11. What do you learn about how to respond to accusers from the way Paul responded to his accusers?

Ask God to give you patience and a heart of love for the people who surround you—your coworkers, your family, people you can show the example of Christ.

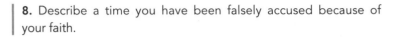

NOW OR LATER

Make a list of at least ten people in your life who do not know and follow Jesus. By each name describe, as best you can, what is keeping them from Jesus. What are ways that you can serve them, get to know them better or spend time with them? Ask God to give you his heart for each of them and to work in their hearts and yours—that you might share the gospel with them.

ELEVEN

TESTIMONY
BEFORE AGRIPPA

Acts 25:13–26:32

I n *Amazing Faith*, the story of Bill Bright's life, there is an account of a survey taken on campuses throughout the United States. The survey asked questions about church attendance and the students' opinions of various religious leaders such as Buddha, Muhammad and Jesus. One of the questions asked was "In your opinion how does one become a Christian?" Ninety-seven percent of the students said that they did not know. When the results were given to Bill Bright, the founder of Campus Crusade for Christ, he said, "They don't know how. They don't know how." He put his head down and sobbed for a long, long time. Like the apostle Paul, Bill Bright's greatest desire was for people to come to know Jesus.

Group Discussion. What motivates you to tell non-Christians about Jesus?

Personal Reflection. To what degree are you concerned about your not-yet-Christian friends becoming Christians?

Though his innocence has been clearly stated many times, Paul remains a prisoner. He repeatedly has to face the unfair charges of the Jewish leaders. He has made his defense with integrity and power, and in return he gets only threats of death. In it all Paul's witness remains consistent. His greatest desire is that his accusers and those in judgment over him will become Christians. *Read Acts 25:13-27.*

1. Describe the nature and content of Festus's report to Agrippa.

2. As is the case with the others who were asked to pronounce judgment on Paul, Festus does not know what to do with Paul. Paul was obviously not guilty or deserving of death or imprisonment. Yet keeping the peace with the Jews was more important to him than justice. Since Festus had already decided what he was going to do with Paul, why do you think he talked to King Agrippa about him?

3. What is the main point about Christianity that Festus mentions?

4. What do you think people most remember about Christianity from your witness?

5. Why do you think King Agrippa wanted to hear Paul?

6. *Read Acts 26.* What are the main points about himself that Paul presents in his defense?

7. Describe the main points of your own coming to Jesus.

8. Why does Paul say that he is on trial (26:6-8)?

9. Contrast the commission of the Sanhedrin (26:9-11) to the commission of Christ (26:15-18).

10. Describe Paul's final interaction with King Agrippa (26:26-29).

11. How does Paul's heart for King Agrippa compare or contrast with your heart for those around you who do not know Christ?

 Praise God for the faithful witness of Paul and others. Thank God specifically for the benefits you have experienced in your relationship with God because of these faithful brothers and sisters.

NOW OR LATER

Write out your story of how you came to Jesus. Include in this a description of the difference that Jesus has made in your life. Practice telling your story to another Christian. Ask God to show you someone who does not know Jesus with whom you can share your story.

TWELVE

PAUL IN ROME!

Acts 27–28

R ome at last!
Paul was innocent. He could have been a free man. But he had
appealed to Caesar—and to Caesar he was to go.

As we look at these last two chapters of Acts and complete our study
of the life of this marvelous servant of God, it might be worthwhile
to ask the questions "Who was really free, and who were the
real prisoners?"

Group Discussion. What do you think it means to be free?

Personal Reflection. Sit quietly for a few moments, without trying to
force your thoughts to move in any direction. Let silence reign in your
heart before you look at Scripture.

In this study Paul offers us a model to go forth to proclaim Jesus boldly.
Read Acts 27–28.

1. Though Paul had every reason by this time to become very self-
centered, how do you see him continue to minister to others
throughout these two chapters (27:9-10, 21-25, 31-38, 42-43; 28:3,
8-9, 17-20, 23-31)?

2. What do you see of Paul's compassion as he ministers?

How do you need to grow in compassion for others?

| **3.** How do you see others minister to Paul throughout this passage?

| **4.** How freely do you allow others to care for and encourage you as you live for Jesus?

| **5.** What do you think it says about Paul that Julius let him go see his friends (27:3)?

| **6.** What do you see of Paul's confidence in God throughout this passage?

| **7.** How were others affected by this great confidence in God?

| **8.** In what ways have you seen your confidence in God affect those around you?

| **9.** In Rome Paul continues to preach under guard. What are the results (28:17-30)?

10. What are the situations or relationships in your life with non-Christians in which you are tempted to give up on your proclamation of the gospel?

11. What truths from this study of Acts encourage you to not give up?

12. The words "boldly and without hindrance he preached the kingdom of God and taught about the Lord Jesus Christ" (28:31) summarize not only Paul's two years in Rome but his whole Christian life. To what degree would you like this to be a summary of your life? Explain.

Thank the Lord for what he has taught you from the book of Acts. Ask him to continue to teach you as you try to live out what you have learned.

NOW OR LATER

Review the book of Acts. Jot down the truths and facts that motivate and equip you to be a witness "to the ends of the earth" (1:8).

As we have looked at God's power in the world and in the church through his Holy Spirit may we go forth from Acts, even as Paul did, "boldly and without hindrance proclaiming the kingdom of God and teaching others about the Lord Jesus Christ."

LEADER'S NOTES

My grace is sufficient for you.

2 CORINTHIANS 12:9

Leading a Bible discussion can be an enjoyable and rewarding experience. But it can also be *scary*—especially if you've never done it before. If this is your feeling, you're in good company. When God asked Moses to lead the Israelites out of Egypt, he replied, "O Lord, please send someone else to do it"! (Ex 4:13). It was the same with Solomon, Jeremiah and Timothy, but God helped these people in spite of their weaknesses, and he will help you as well.

You don't need to be an expert on the Bible or a trained teacher to lead a Bible discussion. The idea behind these inductive studies is that the leader guides group members to discover for themselves what the Bible has to say. This method of learning will allow group members to remember much more of what is said than a lecture would.

These studies are designed to be led easily. As a matter of fact, the flow of questions through the passage from observation to interpretation to application is so natural that you may feel that the studies lead themselves. This study guide is also flexible. You can use it with a variety of groups—student, professional, neighborhood or church groups. Each study takes forty-five to sixty minutes in a group setting.

There are some important facts to know about group dynamics and encouraging discussion. The suggestions listed below should enable you to effectively and enjoyably fulfill your role as leader.

PREPARING FOR THE STUDY

1. Ask God to help you understand and apply the passage in your own life. Unless this happens, you will not be prepared to lead others. Pray too for the various members of the group. Ask God to open your hearts to the message of his Word and motivate you to action.

2. Read the introduction to the entire guide to get an overview of the entire book and the issues which will be explored.

3. As you begin each study, read and reread the assigned Bible passage to familiarize yourself with it.

4. This study guide is based on the New International Version of the Bible. It will help you and the group if you use this translation as the basis for your study and discussion.

5. Carefully work through each question in the study. Spend time in meditation and reflection as you consider how to respond.

6. Write your thoughts and responses in the space provided in the study guide. This will help you to express your understanding of the passage clearly.

7. It might help to have a Bible dictionary handy. Use it to look up any unfamiliar words, names or places. (For additional help on how to study a passage, see chapter five of *How to Lead a LifeGuide Bible Study*, Inter-Varsity Press.)

8. Consider how you can apply the Scripture to your life. Remember that the group will follow your lead in responding to the studies. They will not go any deeper than you do.

9. Once you have finished your own study of the passage, familiarize yourself with the leader's notes for the study you are leading. These are designed to help you in several ways. First, they tell you the purpose the study guide author had in mind when writing the study. Take time to think through how the study questions work together to accomplish that purpose. Second, the notes provide you with additional background information or suggestions on group dynamics for various questions. This information can be useful when people have difficulty understanding or answering a question. Third, the leader's notes can alert you to potential problems you may encounter during the study.

10. If you wish to remind yourself of anything mentioned in the leader's notes, make a note to yourself below that question in the study.

LEADING THE STUDY

1. Begin the study on time. Open with prayer, asking God to help the group to understand and apply the passage.

2. Be sure that everyone in your group has a study guide. Encourage the group to prepare beforehand for each discussion by reading the introduction to the guide and by working through the questions in the study.

3. At the beginning of your first time together, explain that these studies are meant to be discussions, not lectures. Encourage the members of the group to participate. However, do not put pressure on those who may be hesitant to speak during the first few sessions. You may want to suggest the following guidelines to your group.

- Stick to the topic being discussed.

- Your responses should be based on the verses which are the focus of the discussion and not on outside authorities such as commentaries or speakers.

- These studies focus on a particular passage of Scripture. Only rarely should you refer to other portions of the Bible. This allows for everyone to participate in in-depth study on equal ground.

- Anything said in the group is considered confidential and will not be discussed outside the group unless specific permission is given to do so.

- We will listen attentively to each other and provide time for each person present to talk.

- We will pray for each other.

4. Have a group member read the introduction at the beginning of the discussion.

5. Every session begins with a group discussion question. The question or activity is meant to be used before the passage is read. The question introduces the theme of the study and encourages group members to begin to open up. Encourage as many members as possible to participate, and be ready to get the discussion going with your own response.

This section is designed to reveal where our thoughts or feelings need to be transformed by Scripture. That is why it is especially important not to read the passage before the discussion question is asked. The passage will tend to color the honest reactions people would otherwise give because they are, of course, supposed to think the way the Bible does.

You may want to supplement the group discussion question with an icebreaker to help people to get comfortable. See the community section of *Small Group Idea Book* for more ideas.

You also might want to use the personal reflection question with your group. Either allow a time of silence for people to respond individually or discuss it together.

6. Have a group member (or members if the passage is long) read aloud the passage to be studied. Then give people several minutes to read the passage again silently so that they can take it all in.

7. Question 1 will generally be an overview question designed to briefly survey the passage. Encourage the group to look at the whole passage, but try to avoid getting sidetracked by questions or issues that will be addressed later in the study.

8. As you ask the questions, keep in mind that they are designed to be used just as they are written. You may simply read them aloud. Or you may prefer to express them in your own words.

There may be times when it is appropriate to deviate from the study guide. For example, a question may have already been answered. If so, move on to the next question. Or someone may raise an important question not covered in the guide. Take time to discuss it, but try to keep the group from going off on tangents.

9. Avoid answering your own questions. If necessary, repeat or rephrase them until they are clearly understood. Or point out something you read in the leader's notes to clarify the context or meaning. An eager group quickly becomes passive and silent if they think the leader will do most of the talking.

10. Don't be afraid of silence. People may need time to think about the question before formulating their answers.

11. Don't be content with just one answer. Ask, "What do the rest of you think?" or "Anything else?" until several people have given answers to the question.

12. Acknowledge all contributions. Try to be affirming whenever possible. Never reject an answer. If it is clearly off-base, ask, "Which verse led you to that conclusion?" or again, "What do the rest of you think?"

13. Don't expect every answer to be addressed to you, even though this will probably happen at first. As group members become more at ease, they will begin to truly interact with each other. This is one sign of healthy discussion.

14. Don't be afraid of controversy. It can be very stimulating. If you don't resolve an issue completely, don't be frustrated. Move on and keep it in mind for later. A subsequent study may solve the problem.

15. Periodically summarize what the group has said about the passage. This helps to draw together the various ideas mentioned and gives continuity to the study. But don't preach.

16. At the end of the Bible discussion you may want to allow group members a time of quiet to work on an idea under "Now or Later." Then discuss what you experienced. Or you may want to encourage group members to work on these ideas between meetings. Give an opportunity during the session for people to talk about what they are learning.

17. Conclude your time together with conversational prayer, adapting the prayer suggestion at the end of the study to your group. Ask for God's help in following through on the commitments you've made.

18. End on time.

Many more suggestions and helps are found in *How to Lead a Life-Guide Bible Study,* which is part of the LifeGuide Bible Study series.

COMPONENTS OF SMALL GROUPS

A healthy small group should do more than study the Bible. There are four components to consider as you structure your time together.

Nurture. Small groups help us to grow in our knowledge and love of God. Bible study is the key to making this happen and is the foundation of your small group.

Community. Small groups are a great place to develop deep friendships with other Christians. Allow time for informal interaction before and after each study. Plan activities and games that will help you get to know each other. Spend time having fun together—going on a picnic or cooking dinner together.

Worship and prayer. Your study will be enhanced by spending time praising God together in prayer or song. Pray for each other's needs—and keep track of how God is answering prayer in your group. Ask God to help you to apply what you are learning in your study.

Outreach. Reaching out to others can be a practical way of applying what you are learning, and it will keep your group from becoming self-focused. Host a series of evangelistic discussions for your friends or neighbors. Clean up the yard of an elderly friend. Serve at a soup kitchen together, or spend a day working on a Habitat house.

Many more suggestions and helps in each of these areas are found in *Small Group Idea Book.* Information on building a small group can be found in *Small Group Leaders' Handbook* and *The Big Book on Small Groups* (both from InterVarsity Press). Reading through one of these books would be worth your time.

STUDY 1. ACTS 13–14. THE CHARACTER OF EVANGELISM.

PURPOSE: To examine Paul's personal qualities that made him effective in the task of worldwide evangelization.

Question 1. As you lead the group in responding to this question, consider such aspects as starting in the Jewish synagogues on the Sabbath, being led by the Holy Spirit, clearly presenting truth, using Scripture as the basis of all that they said and going where people were open to what they had to say. Also consider the towns they traveled to, the crosscultural emphasis, and the emphasis placed on choosing, encouraging and training leaders. They confronted opposition and evil head on (13:9-11). This is not an exhaustive list. It is here to help you get the group started on picking out the qualities of Paul and Barnabas, but let the members of your group take the lead and add some of the above as you need to.

> The practice of announcing the Christian message first of all in the Jewish synagogue or synagogues of each city they visited was to be a regular feature of Barnabas and Paul's missionary procedure. It was a practical expression of the principle that Paul lays down in Rom. 1:16—that the gospel is to be presented "to the Jew first." Besides, Paul "was always sure of a good opening for his Gentile mission among the 'God-fearing,' who formed part of his audience in every synagogue." (Bruce, *Book of Acts,* p. 263)

They were *sent from* Antioch, which was an important city to
the Roman Empire. It was the cosmopolitan meeting place of Jew,
Greek, Roman and Syrian. . . .

Finally, do not overlook the process in which Barnabas moves
from the driver's seat to the back seat. When the expedition sets
out from Syria, the order is "Barnabas and Saul"; by the time they
leave Cyprus, it is "Paul and his company"!

Barnabas does not seem to have resented this at all. (Bruce,
Book of Acts, p. 266)

This question can go beyond the characteristics seen in this passage
to other qualities that you would like to see the Holy Spirit develop in
yourselves.

Question 3. Antioch was the second great metropolis of the church and
the mother of Gentile Christianity.

The leaders of the church were united and established an atmo-
sphere of worship, prayer and fasting in which they could be sensitive to God's voice and purpose for those in their fellowship.
They were obedient to God and placed hands on Saul and
Barnabas and sent them off, supported and prayed for.

There are indications that NT Christians were especially sensitive to the Spirit's communications during fasting. On this occasion the divine message directed the leaders of the church to set
Barnabas and Saul apart for a special work to which He had called
them. It is perhaps worth noticing that the two men who were to
be released for what we nowadays call missionary service overseas
were the two most eminent and gifted leaders in the church.
(Bruce, *Book of Acts,* p. 261)

The world ministry which thus began was destined to change the
history of Europe and the world.

It is important to recognize and practice what was done in relationship to Saul and Barnabas's call to this ministry as we consider
being called by God to worldwide evangelization. It was in the context
of Christian community that they were called and sent out. We can
assume that this prayer support for them continued throughout the

three years that they were gone. They also were the community to whom Saul and Barnabas were accountable and reported back to.

Question 4. This question is not meant to be a gripe session about churches but to objectively evaluate and possibly help churches move toward change where it is needed. It can certainly be content for prayer.

Question 5. Help your group to look carefully at this message as a means of insight into the gospel but also as a means to begin equipping them to communicate the gospel to those people in their sphere of influence.

"Up to this point, we have had one-line synopses of what Paul said in the synagogues of Damascus and Jerusalem, or to the people in Syrian Antioch. Now as a part of his first missionary journey, we have a chance to be part of the synagogue in Antioch in Phrygia to listen to a comprehensive, theologically developed communication of what Jesus Christ has done to set us free" (Ogilvie, *Communicator's Commentary*, p. 214).

"The history of the Jewish people, Paul maintains, becomes intelligible only in the consummation found in Christ, in whom the promise, given originally to the Jews, found fulfillment. The Law cannot save; it is incomplete (27, 32, 33, 39). This, of course, is the theme of the Epistle to the Galatians. In spite of God's preparation through all history (17-23), and especially through the ministry of the Forerunner (24, 25), the Jews of Jerusalem rejected Him (27-29), but in so doing fulfilled prophecy, and set atonement and resurrection in the gospel (30-41)" (Tasker, *Acts of the Apostles,* p. 105).

Question 6. He begins where they are, with what they know and with their history. They started in the synagogue, the place of worship of the people. They built on what had been read from the Law and the Prophets. He used their own prophets to warn them about what could happen to them.

Question 10. How excited do people get over others becoming Christians? How much is this a part of the concern? How much do we experience the "joy of the Holy Spirit"?

Question 11. Your group may need some time to think about this. Let them have it. Have some examples from your own life to share.

STUDY 2. ACTS 15. CONFLICT IN THE CHURCH.

PURPOSE: To consider ways of handling conflict within the Christian community.

Question 1. Set the stage for this drama. Who is there? What are the circumstances of this conflict?

Questions 2-3. Look carefully and help the group to respond fully to this question. Conflict within the Christian community is a great enemy of the church today because it is often not dealt with biblically. The response to this question is the base for question 4, observing principles that are vital in conflict resolution today, and question 6—where do I need help? The first step was acknowledging that there was conflict. It was not glossed over. There was an open spirit to deal with the conflict. They sent people up to Jerusalem where the conflict began.

They focused on God rather than on the conflict. As Paul and Barnabas went up to Jerusalem, they told people of all the wonderful works of God. That was what they started with upon arriving in Jerusalem.

The believers in Jerusalem "welcomed" them. They did not begrudge their coming. There was no reserve or resentment. They were all open to listening to each other as well as sharing their perspective in a loving way. They spoke from their experience of seeing God work among the Gentiles, and they spoke from the Word of God. They realized the necessity that the Word and their experience were in agreement.

Their desire as a body was to encourage the new Gentile converts. They loved them. They responded to them and directed them. They spoke openly of their brotherhood with the Gentile believers. They did not lord seniority or position over them. They demonstrated the importance of the new believers by sending people to encourage them and to communicate with them, as well as a letter.

The new believers were encouraged. They then separated in peace. They hadn't forced on the new Christians a pattern of behavior that was nonessential to being a Christian.

Question 6. They were each deeply dedicated to the service of Christ. They were as one in their determination to take God's love to the world and in their doctrinal belief. They agreed that it was a good idea to visit the churches they had planted and even that they needed another team member. Their history which we have observed up to this point would speak of a strong base of relationship and unity.

Question 8. Finding a temporary solution is better than continued warfare. It allowed them to continue to serve the Lord. There were two teams that went out instead of one. It gave time for the two of them to more thoroughly seek God's mind for a solution.

We have reason to believe from Scripture that Paul and Barnabas were reconciled (1 Cor 9:6; Gal 2:11-13; 2 Tim 4:11). Their not-so-perfect short-term solution made it possible for healing in the long run.

Question 10. We are short sighted human beings. Though we certainly should have strong convictions and be able to communicate those to others, the way we do that communicating is very important. Horace Fenton Jr., in his book *When Christians Clash* (Downers Grove, Ill.: Inter-Varsity Press, 1987), speaks of "advancing our arguments against fellow Christians with what one wise man paradoxically called 'tentative finality.'" The fact that Paul and Barnabas did not have a full picture should not have silenced them, but it should have reminded them of their fallibility.

STUDY 3. ACTS 16. WHAT MUST I DO?

PURPOSE: To understand the significance of immediate and unreserved obedience to the call of God.

General note. "It was Timothy's mixed parentage that made Paul decide to circumcise him before taking him along as a travel companion. In the eyes of Jews, Timothy was a Gentile because he was the uncircumcised son of a Greek. In Gentile eyes, however, he was practically a Jew, having been brought up in his mother's religion. Paul therefore regularized his status (and in Jewish eyes, legitimized him) by circumcising him" (Bruce, *Book of Acts*, p. 322).

Timothy was not required to be circumcised. The council at Jerusalem had already decided this. But he voluntarily did this to overcome any barriers to his witness for Christ.

Help your group to think through what it means to be guided by God. It is important to be willing at any time to lay aside our own plans, as good and well intentioned as they may be, in response to the Spirit's prompting. Though Paul had a thoughtful plan of action and travel, he changed those without apparent question when told by the Spirit on two different occasions not to go somewhere. Here are other principles of guidance: ask God to open and close doors of circumstances to lead you; pray continually about plans and direction; talk with mature, godly Christians; check out your internal motivation for taking such actions; and make sure your plan is true to the principles in God's Word. And finally, be ready for God to speak to you in whatever way he chooses. He will lead not only in the direction he wants us to take but also away from the wrong direction or situation.

Question 5. Opposition to the truth of the gospel today can be very overt or quite subtle. It can come from both Christians and non-Christians—very subtly when from Christians. It can take the form of physical, emotional and spiritual persecution. The reasons can be such things as material gain, social status, threat to other religions and dogma, or fear of what response and obedience to the gospel might mean in a person's life.

Question 6. Lead the group in looking carefully at the whole story of the conversion of the Philippian jailer. Discuss all the details that could have influenced the jailer to come to the Lord, from the attitudes of Paul and Silas to the earthquake to the miracle of all the prisoners still being present. Examine all the possible ways that God chose to work in this situation.

Question 9. F. F. Bruce offers this analysis:

Three individuals are singled out by Luke among Paul's converts at Philippi, and they differ so much one from another that he might be thought to have deliberately selected them in order to show how the saving name of Jesus proved its power in the lives of the most diverse types of men and women. The first is Lydia, the independent business-woman of reputable character and God-fearing mind; as she heard the gospel story, "the Lord opened her heart to give heed to what was said by Paul" (RSV). But the second is a person of a very different stamp: an unfortunate demon-possessed slave-girl, whose owners exploited her infirmity for their material profit. She is described by Luke as a "pythoness", *i.e.* as a person inspired by Apollo, the god particularly associated with the giving of oracles, who was worshipped as the "Pythian" god at the oracular shrine of Delphi (otherwise called Pytho) in central Greece. Her involuntary utterances were regarded as the voice of the god, and she was thus much in demand by people who wished to have their fortunes told.

Her deliverance demanded much more spectacular measures than did Lydia's quiet turning in heart to the Lord. Day by day, as the missionaries went to the place of prayer, she followed them through the streets of Philippi, advertising them aloud as servants of the Most High God, who proclaimed the way of salvation. The title, "Most High God," was one which provided Jews and Gentiles with a convenient common denominator for the Supreme Being, and "salvation" in the religious sense was as eagerly sought by Gentiles as by Jews.

The missionaries, however, did not appreciate her "unsolicited testimonials", and at last Paul, vexed by her continual clamour, exorcized the spirit that possessed her, commanding it in the name of Jesus Christ to come out of her. The words had scarcely left his lips before she was released from her familiar spirit. (Bruce, *Book of Acts*, pp. 332-33)

The final convert, quite different from both of the women, was a jailer who embraced the message of salvation with joy. The gospel was affecting all levels of society.

STUDY 4. ACTS 17. AN UNKNOWN GOD.

PURPOSE: To observe how Paul understands and responds to the different cultures to which he is communicating the gospel, and to be motivated to understand the people and culture of those to whom God has called us to minister.

Group discussion. This is a good time to look at the modern-day philosophies that are thriving in our world. Consider such things as the New Age, Eastern mysticism, Satan worship, the occult world, humanism, liberalism and others.

Question 1. The second question is an overview to lead the group to look over the whole passage.

> In accordance with his regular practice, (in Thessalonica) Paul
> visited the local synagogue, and (having probably been asked to
> speak, as previously at Pisidian Antioch) he expounded the OT
> scriptures on three successive sabbath days, bringing forward as
> evidence of their fulfillment the historic facts accomplished in the
> ministry, death and exaltation of Jesus, setting the fulfillment
> alongside the predictions in order that the force of his argument
> might be readily grasped. According to these predictions, the
> Messiah was appointed to suffer and then to rise from the dead;
> both these experiences had been fulfilled in Jesus of Nazareth
> (and in nobody else); therefore, said he, "this is the Messiah, this
> Jesus whom I am proclaiming to you." (Bruce, *Book of Acts,* p. 343)

In Thessalonica some Jews believed, and more God-fearing Greeks believed. Some of the Jews who did not believe were incensed and began rioting against Paul and his companions. They were accused of revolutionary activity against the Roman Empire.

"The apostles proclaimed the kingdom of God, a very different kingdom from any secular empire, and no doubt they gave Jesus the Greek title basileus ('king'), by which the Roman Emperor was described by his Greek speaking subjects" (Bruce, *Book of Acts,* p. 345).

In Berea Paul again began in the synagogue, but the reception given by the Jewish community was far different than that in Thessalonica.

> For, with commendable open-mindedness, they brought the
> claims made by Paul to the touchstone of Holy Writ instead of
> giving way to prejudice. Their procedure, "examining the scrip-
> tures daily to see if these things were so" (RSV), is worthy of imi-
> tation by all who have some new form of religious teaching
> pressed upon their acceptance. These Beroean Jews could not
> have foreseen how many Christian groups of later days would call
> themselves "Beroeans" after their worthy example of Bible study.
> As we might expect from people who welcomed the apostolic
> message with such eagerness of mind, many of them believed. As
> at Thessalonica, the believers included many God-fearing Greeks,

both men and women, and some of these—particularly the women—belonged to the leading families in the city." (Bruce, *Book of Acts*, p. 347)

Question 3. "Athens was not exactly on Paul's missionary programme, and during the days that he waited there for his two friends to rejoin him, he had leisure to walk round the violet-crowned city and view its masterpieces of architecture and sculpture.

"Athens, although she had long since lost her political eminence of an earlier day, continued to represent the highest level of culture attained in classical antiquity. The sculpture, literature and oratory of Athens in the fifth and fourth centuries B.C. have, indeed, never been surpassed. In philosophy, too, she occupied the leading place, being the native city of Socrates and Plato, and the adopted home of Aristotle, Epicurus and Zeno. In all these fields Athens retained unchallenged prestige, and her political glory as the cradle of democracy was not completely dimmed. In consideration of her splendid past, the Romans left Athens free to carry on her own institutions as a free and allied city within the Roman Empire. . . .

"Whatever Paul may have felt in the way of artistic appreciation, the feeling that was uppermost in his mind as he walked here and there in Athens was one of indignation: the beautiful city was 'full of idols,' dedicated to the worship of gods which were no gods—for 'the things which the Gentiles sacrifice, they sacrifice to demons and not to God' (1 Cor. 10:20)" (Bruce, *Book of Acts*, pp. 348-49).

If Paul's strategy of worldwide evangelization doesn't come up in discussion, you might want to point out to the group that we see continued evidence of it here. It is good and right to have a plan. And with a plan it is still possible to be led by the Spirit of God. (This ministry in Athens was not in Paul's original plan.) These are not opposed to each other.

It is also evident here that all truth is God's truth. In verse 28 Paul quotes a pagan poet to make one of his points.

Paul spends much of his time here in the marketplace and was even taken to a meeting of the Court of Areopagus, which "retained authority in matters of religion and morals, and in Roman times it enjoyed enhanced power and commanded great respect" (Bruce, *Book of Acts*, p. 352).

It was before this court that Paul was brought to give an account of his philosophy. Note that instead of beginning with Scripture, he begins with statements and items that are familiar to the people. He talks about their being religious. He mentions their objects of worship and an altar with the inscription "TO AN UNKNOWN GOD." From that point he tells them about the true living God.

Questions 6-7. Help the group not to gloss over these questions. As the leader, you should think ahead of time through modern objects of worship and how the message of Christ speaks to them. Some objects of worship are material goods, status, personal identity, jobs, our country, our military power and our own strength.

Question 8. Some "points of truth" include beginning where people might be, fear of death, non-nurturing families, "Jesus was a good man," "I am what I do" and so forth.

Question 11. Compromise of the gospel can be subtle and unintentional. Sometimes we are so acculturated we do not even realize the truth is being watered down. Do we communicate with conviction, though with great compassion, that repentance is essential for salvation? Is the message of the resurrected Lord proclaimed loudly and clearly? Do we skirt the issue of sin? We must not compromise the message of Jesus Christ, but we must be full of love and tenderness as we communicate this message clearly.

STUDY 5. ACTS 18. COMPANIONS IN MINISTRY.

PURPOSE: To be reminded of the strategic role that relationships with others play in our motivation for and efforts to evangelize.

Question 1. Limit the time spent on this question. This is an overview question. The passage should simply be scanned and the people listed, giving a sense of how many people there are in Paul's life.

Question 2. "This married couple, whom Paul later called his 'fellow-workers in Christ Jesus', who had 'risked their lives' for him, exemplified an extraordinary degree of mobility. They left Rome for Corinth. They later undertook a further move, this time from Corinth to Ephesus in the company of Paul, and the church, or a portion of it, met in their house (18:18, 19, 26).

"Each Jewish boy learned a trade and tried to earn his living with it. Paul and Aquila had been trained in tentmaking. As a tentmaker Paul was able to go wherever God led him carrying his livelihood with him" (*Life Application Bible,* p. 1669).

To summarize the significance of Aquila and Priscilla's relationship with Paul: they provided him a place to stay, earned a living together, possibly supported him financially (one commentator suggests that they might have financed his trip to Ephesus), traveled with him, shared their home with the church and participated in his ministry. Paul was sustained by their faithful friendship.

Question 3. "After a few weeks, Paul was rejoined by his colleagues Silas and Timothy. The news that they brought from Macedonia (especially Timothy's news about the steadfastness of the sorely-tried converts of Thessalonica) was a great relief to Paul; and a gift of money which they brought him from his friends in Philippi relieved him for the time being of the necessity to support himself by leatherworking; he was able therefore to concentrate on the preaching of the gospel, as he sought to convince the Jewish community that Jesus was the true Messiah" (Bruce, *Book of Acts,* pp. 370-71). Their sheer faithfulness in travel and ministry must have been a great encouragement to Paul.

Questions 7-8. "Shortly after Paul left the synagogue and made the house of Titius Justus his headquarters, he had an encouraging experience—he received one of the visions which came to him at critical periods in his life, heartening him for the work that lay ahead. In this particular vision the risen Christ appeared to him by night and assured him that no harm would befall him in Corinth, for the opposition that his preaching might stir up. He should therefore abandon any fear that he might have, and go on proclaiming the gospel boldly; he would reap an abundant harvest by so doing, for the Lord had many people in Corinth whom He had marked out for His own.

"Thus filled with fresh confidence, Paul stayed in Corinth and continued his work of proclamation and teaching for eighteen months" (Bruce, *Book of Acts,* p. 372).

Question 9. We have already discussed the significance of Paul's relationship with Aquila and Priscilla. Very probably his hair being cut off was also connected in some way to his relationships with people. Concerning the vow that was made:

> The reference to his hair makes it almost certain that it was a Nazirite vow, which involved abstinence from drinking wine and from cutting one's hair for a period, at the end of which the hair was first cut and then burned, along with other sacrifices as a symbol of self-offering to God. If the vow was completed away from Jerusalem, the hair could still be brought there to be burned. Such vows were made either in thankfulness for past blessings (such as Paul's safe keeping in Corinth) or as a part of a petition for future blessings (such as safe keeping on Paul's impending journey). Once Paul had been liberated from the attempt to be justified by the law, his conscience was free to take part in practices which, being ceremonial or cultural, belonged to the matters indifferent, perhaps on this occasion in order to conciliate the Jewish Christian leaders he was going to see in Jerusalem. (Stott, *Message of Acts,* pp. 300-301)

We see his continued commitment to the Jews, though they are very difficult. In this situation they seem more responsive and even ask him to come back. He promises to do so if it is the Lord's will.

Though few words tell about it in this portion of Scripture (vv. 22-23), Paul's relationship to the church is important to them and to him. He spent time with them, shared with them and strengthened the disciples.

Question 11. When it was evident that Apollos's teaching was defective and that he needed more training, Aquila and Priscilla invited him to their home and explained the way of God more accurately.

"Their ministry was timely and discreet. As Professor Bruce remarks, 'how much better it is to give such private help to a preacher whose ministry is defective than to correct him or denounce him publicly'" (Stott, *Message of Acts,* p. 296).

"Next, when Apollos wanted to go to Achaia, the brothers encouraged him, for he was better equipped now for a wider ministry, and wrote to the disciples there to welcome him. On arriving, he vigorously refuted the Jews in public debate, proving from the Scriptures that Jesus was the Christ. Indeed in 1 Corinthians 1-4 Paul himself wrote appreciatively of Apollos' ministry in Corinth and generously acknowledged him as a fellow worker in God's field. 'I planted the seed,' he wrote; 'Apollos watered it, but God made it grow'" (Stott, *Message of Acts*, p. 303).

STUDY 6. ACTS 19:1–20:12. IN THE NAME OF JESUS.

PURPOSE: To see the different types of reactions as the power of God is demonstrated in mighty ways. To be motivated to seek the demonstration of this power in our lives and Christian communities.

General note. Ephesus was the capital and leading business center of the Roman province of Asia. It is part of present-day Turkey. Because it was a hub of transportation, both sea and land, it ranked with the greatness of Antioch and Alexandria. It was a major city on the Mediterranean Sea.

Group discussion. God's power is revealed in all sorts of ways—from his giving wisdom for dealing with a child to the miracle of the new birth to reconciliation in a broken relationship to supernatural healing. This question is simply meant to prepare the group for considering God's power and the effects of it on the world.

Question 1. This question is to serve as an overview of the passage. Help set the pace for just scanning the passage. However, help the group to see not just the dramatic episodes as the power of God in action, but such powerful things as a person believing in Jesus. Some of the episodes will be discussed in more detail as we move through the study.

Question 2. This is another overview question. Watch your time.

Question 4. This question should bring out the fact that Paul met a small group of people with a particular spiritual need—to receive the Holy Spirit—and effectively met that need. He began by asking sensitive questions. He started where they were, and where they had been, and then took them a step forward in their growth and spiritual experience. They were receptive and responsive.

This episode, depending on the makeup of your group, has potential for being controversial. Try to avoid the controversy and stay with what all can agree upon. The commentary material below might be helpful if controversy cannot be avoided. Even so, at some point it might be necessary for you to say, "Let's move on with our study and discuss this point after our study is over."

Some feel this text is proof that conversion occurs in steps. First there is repentance and a commitment to Jesus, and then a second step in which one receives the Holy Spirit. Others believe that this all takes place at one time with conversion. This debate cannot be settled (and minds will most likely not be changed) in the process of this study. There are some issues where Christians have to agree to disagree and move on.

> John's baptism was a sign of repentance from sin only, not a sign of new life in Christ. Like Apollos (18:24-26), these Ephesian believers needed further instruction on the message and ministry of Jesus Christ. By faith they believed in Jesus as the Messiah, but they did not understand the significance of Jesus' death and resurrection or the work of the Holy Spirit. Therefore they had not experienced the presence and power of the Holy Spirit.
>
> In the book of Acts, believers received the Holy Spirit in a variety of ways. Usually the Holy Spirit filled a person as soon as he or she professed faith in Christ. In this case, however, God allowed it to happen later. God was confirming to these believers who did not initially know about the Holy Spirit that they too were a part of the church. The Holy Spirit's filling endorsed them as believers.
>
> Pentecost was the formal outpouring of the Holy Spirit to the church. The other outpourings in the book of Acts were God's way of uniting new believers to the church. The mark of the true church is not merely right doctrine, but evidence of the Holy Spirit's work. (*Life Application Bible,* p. 1673)

Question 5. We need to ask questions more. We need to allow others to tell us where they are in their relationship with God. We need to take seriously what they share and then begin our communication from where they are and according to their openness. The disciples were ready for what Paul had to offer. He forced nothing on them. More time should be spent listening to others than talking.

Question 6. Paul patiently and faithfully began his ministry in the synagogue as he had in other cities. He knew the Jews at Ephesus from his previous visit when they had pressed him to stay longer. He had promised to come back if God willed. But the old patterns continued and the Jewish leaders rejected the message. Paul took up residence in a secular environment in the teaching hall of Tyrannus. Those who had accepted his message in the synagogue could follow him there.

Notice that for two full years this work went on. Paul stayed in Ephesus, but his colleagues worked out in other cities. Verse 10 says that everyone had heard the Word of God by the end of that period.

"The province was intensively evangelized, and became one of the leading centres of Christianity for centuries afterwards" (Bruce, *Book of Acts*, p. 389).

Question 7. Too often we have strategies and plans for all types of things in our lives—for our jobs, homes, social lives, goals for the future and our children. But when it comes to one of the most important areas of our lives, that of evangelism, we have no such plans or strategies. What do you need to be thinking, planning and praying about concerning the spread of the gospel in your work place, in your neighborhood and in social or professional groups? How might you penetrate these with the gospel—even to the possible desired end that "all the Jews and Greeks who lived in the province of Asia heard the Word of the Lord"?

Question 8. It has been revealed through scrolls that "pagan" exorcisms took place using the name of Jesus. So Jesus' name was being used by those who didn't follow him—apparently just for power's sake.

Question 13. Just being aware that such negative responses will take place helps us not to be alarmed when it happens. For instance, it is not necessarily bad if someone gets angry when confronted with the gospel. It could mean that the message is getting through. Of course, we need to make sure the anger is not the result of an inappropriate or insensitive approach. Knowing that truth is often copied alerts us to watch for that and warns us not to get caught up in compromise.

Being in tune with God and saturated in his Word is vital preparation. We need his wisdom and insight. We need his comfort and encouragement. We need to be reminded of his purpose and priorities. When the response is positive, we need to give God the full credit and glory for all that is accomplished. Apart from the power of his Spirit we can do nothing.

STUDY 7. ACTS 20:13-38. SAYING GOODBYE.

PURPOSE: To review Paul's life and to be motivated by it to strive to complete the task of testifying to God's grace.

Group discussion. This is a dramatic, touching and emotional episode. Paul is saying goodbye to people that he has loved and invested in for three intense years. He has brought them to Christ. He has nurtured and discipled them. He has turned over to them the leadership of the church at Ephesus. And now he knows and is communicating to them that they will never see his face again.

They were grieving. But because this is the last time they will see him, the power of his words increases. They will remember what Paul said. This approach question is to help the group get into the spirit and the emotion of this powerful passage.

Question 1. Not often do we start looking at the content of a passage with a feeling question. However, as in much of life, if not all, the feelings will enrich and emphasize the impact of the content. Scan the passage with this question, but do not rush. However, keep in mind that the content will be covered in more depth as we move through the passage.

"The meeting at Miletus between Paul and the elders of the Ephesian church is important because it contains the one record in Acts of Paul's addressing a Christian audience. The address throws light both on the course of events in the recent past and on Paul's misgivings for the future, although nothing shifted him from his determination to carry out the work divinely allotted to him and to finish his work with joy" (*New Bible Commentary,* 3rd ed., p. 1001).

Question 2. The goal of this study is to review Paul's life and to be motivated by it to strive to complete the task that God has called us to testify to the gospel of God's grace. That means the reviewing of his ministry is very important and the foundation to the rest of the study. Look at each portion carefully.

Question 3. Help the group to respond to this question. The best way is to be prepared to share your response to it. The goal is not to be like Paul.

It is to be us but with the same motivation and desire for obedience as Paul.

Question 4. Help the group to be specific.

Questions 8-9. "And now he was leaving them; they could no longer count upon his personal presence for such pastoral guidance and wise admonition. But, though Paul might go, God was ever with them, and so was God's word which they had received—the word that proclaimed His grace in redeeming them and His grace in sanctifying them. To God, then, and to this word of His, Paul solemnly committed them. By that word, as they accepted and obeyed it, they would be built up in faith and love together with their fellow-Christians; by that word, too, they were assured of their inheritance among all the people of God, sanctified by His grace. In due time Paul and all the apostles passed from earthly life; but the apostolic teaching which they left behind as a sacred deposit to be guarded by their successors, preserved not merely in the memory of their hearers but in the scriptures of the NT canon, remains with us this day as the Word of God's grace. And those are most truly in the apostolic succession who receive this apostolic teaching, along with the rest of Holy Writ, as their rule of faith and practice" (Bruce, *Book of Acts,* pp. 417-18).

Question 10. You might begin this question with a statement about the importance of the job you are called to do.

> Upon these elders, then lay a solemn responsibility. The Holy Spirit had entrusted them with the charge of the people of God in Ephesus: they had to care for them as shepherds for their flock. . . .
>
> Their responsibility was all the greater in that the congregation of God which He had purchased for Himself (an echo this of O.T. language)—and the ransom price was nothing less than the life-blood of his beloved son. (Bruce, *Book of Acts,* pp. 415-16)

STUDY 8. ACTS 21:1–22:21. FACING OPPOSITION.

PURPOSE: To seek for our lives the single-mindedness of Paul in obedience to God's will.

Question 1. Paul did not disobey the Holy Spirit by going to Jerusalem (v. 4). The Spirit warned the believers about what Paul would suffer there, and they decided he should not go because of that. In the same way the people in verse 12 begged him not to go after hearing the prophecy from Agabus.

Paul knew that he would be imprisoned in Jerusalem. Though no one wants to endure pain, as a faithful disciple Paul wanted above all else to obey God. You might also ask, "What was the source of his resolve (v. 13)?" It is important to note that his resolve centered upon the name of the Lord Jesus Christ.

Question 4. "When the delegates called on James and the elders of the Jerusalem church they were welcomed; but these good men were clearly troubled because of the exaggerated rumours that had reached Jerusalem about Paul's attitude to the law. They admitted that the position with regard to Gentile believers had been defined at the apostolic Council, but they wished Paul to give the lie in a practical manner to the report that he was dissuading *Jewish* Christians from keeping the law and from circumcising their children. Paul himself, so far as we can tell, continued to observe the law throughout his life, especially in Jewish company, and his consent to take the advice of James on this occasion and share the purificatory ceremony of four men who had taken a temporary Nazirite vow and pay their expenses was entirely in keeping with his settled principle: 'To the Jews I became as a Jew, in order to win Jews'" (*New Bible Commentary,* 3rd ed., p. 1002).

Question 5. The *Life Application Bible* offers the following insight:

> The Jerusalem Council (Acts 15) settled the issue of circumcision of Gentile believers. Evidently there was a rumor that Paul had gone far beyond their decision, even forbidding Jews to circumcise their children. This, of course, was not true. So Paul willingly submitted to Jewish custom to show that he was not working against the council's decision and that he was still Jewish in his lifestyle. Sometimes we must go the second mile to avoid offending others, especially when offending them would hinder the gospel.

Paul submitted himself to this Jewish custom to keep peace in the Jerusalem church. Although Paul was a man of strong conviction, he was willing to compromise on nonessential points, becoming all things to all men that he might win some (1 Corinthians 9:19-23). Often a church will split on disagreements about minor issues or traditions. Like Paul, we should remain firm on Christian essentials but flexible on nonessentials. This is exercising the gift of mutual submission for the sake of the gospel. (p. 1680)

Question 6. "It was a remarkable feat of intellectual balance and self-control after the violence of the mob's man handling, and a rescue which can have taken little thought of gentleness, to lay hold of the opportunity for testimony, and in the act assess the needs of the situation and the appropriate approach. Paul casts aside all theology and bases his defense on the facts of personal experience. In spite of the stinging injustice he had suffered, and the ungodly violence of the crowd's attack from which he was still reeling, he does all he possibly can do to conciliate his hostile audience" (Tasker, *Acts of the Apostles,* p. 173).

Question 9. Consider such things as respect, honesty, straightfor-wardness, identification with the listeners and lifting Jesus up.

Bible translators disagree as to whether Paul was speaking Aramaic or Hebrew. However, as Aramaic is derived from Hebrew and was the primary language of Palestinian Jews (*NIV Study Bible,* p. 1689) the following comments are helpful in any case:

Paul was speaking in Hebrew, the language of the Old Testament. He spoke this language not only to communicate in the language of his listeners, but also to show that he was a devout Jew, had respect for the Jewish laws and customs and was learned in Hebrew. Paul spoke Greek to the Roman officials and Hebrew to the Jews. If you want to minister to people with maximum effectiveness, you must be able to use their language.

Gamaliel was the most honored rabbi of the first century. He was well known and respected as an expert on religious law and as a voice for moderation. Paul was showing his credentials as a well-educated man trained under the most respected Jewish rabbi.

When Paul said "just as you have tried to do today (i.e., as any of you are today [NIV])" he acknowledged their sincere motives in trying to kill him and recognized that he would have done the same to Christian leaders a few years earlier. Paul always tried to establish a common point of contact with his audience before launching into a full-scale defense of Christianity. (*Life Application Bible*, p. 1681)

He postpones the name Gentile as long as possible, demonstrating a sensitivity to his audience. He even modifies the Lord's words (Acts 9:15).

"He was bound to speak, however, to speak the whole truth, and there came a place in his address, as there did at Athens, when no art of oratory or grace of language could cover up the point of thrust of the speaker's challenge" (Tasker, *Acts of the Apostles*, pp. 173-74).

STUDY 9. ACTS 22:22–23:35. GOD AT WORK.

PURPOSE: To see God's hand in the life of Paul directing and protecting him in order for God's will to be done. To become more astute at seeing God's hand in our lives and circumstances.

Question 1. This is an overview question. Be aware of time, but also encourage the members to get into the drama of the passage and into all that is so rapidly and intensely happening in Paul's life.

Question 2. This question is intentionally broad. Give the group members time to respond to specific portions or details of this passage that impress or affect them. Be prepared to share yourself.

Question 3. It is God's will for Paul to go to Rome. He is faithfully working this out by both protecting and directing Paul.

"Twice more in this brief section Roman law and justice come to Paul's aid. First Claudius Lysias again rescues him from lynching, and secondly, having discovered his Roman citizenship, from flogging. . . .

"Paul was actually being prepared for the flogging when he divulged his Roman citizenship. Similarly, in Philippi he had not revealed that he was a Roman citizen until after he had been beaten, imprisoned and put in the stocks (16:31). He seems for some reason not to have wanted to take advantage of being a citizen except in some dire extremity" (Stott, *Message of Acts*, pp. 348-50).

Question 4. The disagreement between the Sadducees and the Pharisees and the uproar that it caused led to Paul's being swooped away to protection by the commander.

Question 5. "It is true that the event on the Damascus road shattered and rebuilt Paul's life. Never was conversion so complete and so transforming. But it is also correct to say, as Ramsay maintains that, when Paul came to look over the whole course of his life, and to reflect calmly on the plan which was so clearly woven into it, he saw the continuity and unfolding purpose to which he often makes reference. He had been separated, he claims, from his mother's womb for the task before him. 'Brethren,' he said, 'I have lived in all good conscience before God until this day'" (Tasker, *Acts of the Apostles,* pp. 175-76). Paul was claiming to be serving God sincerely and without offense. His life had been consistently directed to one end—glorifying the God of Israel.

Question 6. Hopefully by this point in the study your group has been together long enough and trust is built enough to not have to put on pretensions so you can discuss this issue honestly.

Question 7. Paul was spared from the plot by the Jews to kill him because of the information brought to him by his nephew.

> On the one hand, the Jewish persecutors were prejudiced and violent. On the other, the Romans were open-minded and went out of their way to maintain the standards of law, justice and order of which their best leaders were understandably proud. Four times they rescued Paul from death either by lynching or murder, taking him into custody until the charges against him could be clarified and, if cogent, presented in court. Then three times in Luke's narrative, as we have seen, Paul either has been or will be declared innocent. (Stott, *Message of Acts,* p. 356)

Question 8. "Paul had passed through two days of fearful mental, spiritual, and physical stress. Twice the intervention of a Roman military patrol had rescued him from the violence of his own compatriots. He was no doubt assailed with misgivings, and the recollection of the warnings which had punctuated his journey to Jerusalem would arise to torment him" (Tasker, *Acts of the Apostles,* p. 177). He needed God's voice of comfort and encouragement.

Question 10. "Lysias somewhat manipulated the facts in order to portray himself in the most favourable light, putting his discovery that Paul was a Roman citizen before his rescue instead of after it, and drawing a discreet veil of silence over his serious offence in binding, and preparing to torture, a Roman citizen. Nine of the principal verbs in his letter are in the first person singular. The letter was fairly honourable, but decidedly self-centered" (Stott, *Message of Acts*, p. 356).

STUDY 10. ACTS 24:1–25:12. FALSELY ACCUSED.

PURPOSE: To learn from Paul how to respond when falsely accused due to our faith.

Group discussion. If you don't get much response—or if the responses don't seem realistic—as a follow-up, you might try, "What if the accusations are made over and over again?"

Question 1. "The charges made followed those levelled against Christ Himself, and fall similarly under three heads. First, Paul was *a pestilent* fellow, and a mover of sedition among all the Jews throughout the world (5). This amounted to a charge of treason.... Secondly, Paul was set down as a ringleader of the Nazarenes, a group without official recognition, and by implication dissident and rebellious. Finally, he had profaned the temple, the one charge on which the Jews appear to have been able even to put a Roman to death. Tertullus backed his accusations with the testimony of eyewitnesses (9)" (Tasker, *Acts of the Apostles*, p. 180).

Question 2. "A few words only of Tertullus' elaborate oration are given, but enough to reveal the nature of this rhetoric and the character of his accusation. Luke has a remarkable aptitude for using thus a brief quotation. It is not unlikely that the orator was a Roman, for there is a Latin ring about some of his phrases as they appear in Luke's Greek, and his name, although this does not necessarily indicate nationality, is Latin. He was certainly trained in the arts of contemporary rhetoric, and what impressed Luke was his elaborate exorduim, a *captatio benevolentiae,* or 'seeking of good will,' as the theorists termed it. Such a subterfuge, says Calvin, is 'a sign of bad conscience'" (Tasker, *Acts of the Apostles*, p. 179).

Question 4. This is a speculative question, though certainly worth thinking about. "Felix had been governor for six years and would have known about the Christians, a topic of conversation among the Roman leaders. The Christians' peaceful lifestyles had shown the Romans that Christians didn't go around starting riots" (*Life Application Bible*, p. 1686).

Question 5. It would seem that Paul's message got too personal, and Felix fell under conviction. Felix had taken another man's wife. When Paul spoke on righteousness, self-control and judgment he became uncomfortable and ended the discussion. There is no evidence that it ever became convenient for Felix to further discuss Christianity.

Question 6. When exposed to truth that reveals sin, some people move further away, even as some are moved by the Holy Spirit to respond in repentance. They might say, as Felix did, "When it is more convenient, I will consider the gospel." That time usually does not come.

   "Many people will be glad to discuss the gospel with you as long as it doesn't touch their lives too personally. When it does some will resist or run away. But this is what the gospel is all about—God's power to change lives" (*Life Application Bible,* p. 1686).

   The gospel's real effectiveness is when it moves from principles and doctrine into a life changing dynamic. When someone resists or runs from your witness, it is possibly because the gospel has become personal.

Question 7. Help the group to look carefully at the passage to find the hints that Festus knows that Paul is innocent. Early in his experience with the Jewish religious leaders Festus says, "If he has done anything wrong" (25:5). He probably knew of Paul's story and reputation too. He knew the charges could not be proven. He does not force Paul to go to Jerusalem to stand trial. He was very eager to send him off to Caesar.

Question 8. Note this question is not the same as the group discussion question. It asks when have you been falsely accused because of your faith.

Question 11. "Striving to keep our conscience clear before God and man" is a vital element in responding to false accusation.

STUDY 11. ACTS 25:13–26:32. TESTIMONY BEFORE AGRIPPA.

PURPOSE: To make Paul's burning desire, that each person will hear the gospel and will become a Christian, our own.

Question 1. I believe Festus's report to Agrippa shows us some of Festus's responses to Paul. It is significant that Paul made an impression on Festus. Though it is important to him to stay on the "good side" of the Jews, he was not ready to ignore Paul's innocence. He was willing to admit to another leader that he did not know what to do. His report made Agrippa want to hear from Paul.

There are many times we may think our witness has no effect. Sometimes, even though we cannot see what is going on with people's inner lives, God is working in them through us.

Question 2. "A fresh difficulty now presented itself to Festus. When he sent Paul to Rome to have his case heard before the emperor, it would be necessary for him to send a report of the case as it had developed up to that time. This was by no means an easy thing to do, especially as Festus could not grasp how the trouble had really started. Listening to the speeches for the prosecution and the defense only added to his perplexity.

"Fortunately for Festus, a way out of this minor difficulty soon appeared. To the north-east of his province lay the petty kingdom which was ruled by Herod Agrippa II. . . .

"Agrippa the younger had the reputation of being an authority on the Jewish religion, and Festus decided that he was the man who could best help him to frame the report which he had to remit to Rome in connection with Paul's appeal to the emperor. So at the suitable opportunity during Agrippa's stay in the provincial capital, Festus broached the subject of Paul's case to him" (Bruce, *Book of Acts,* pp. 481-82).

Knowing Paul was innocent and observing the power of Paul's message ate away at Festus. He could not help but talk about it.

Question 3. Festus says that the issue of controversy seemed to be over Jesus who was dead but whom Paul affirmed to be alive.

Question 4. Help your group to be honest by sharing honestly yourself. Help the group to look at the positive as well as negative responses. The point of the question is not to beat up on one's self but to evaluate, grow and be motivated to change by what we are exposed to in Scripture.

Question 5. This is definitely a speculative question but one worth looking at. Look at all the possibilities that group members can think of. "Agrippa no doubt knew enough about the Christian movement to have his interest whetted by Festus" (Bruce, *Book of Acts,* p. 482).

Question 7. Obviously you cannot hear everyone's complete story. It will be good to hear some of the basic elements of some of the stories of members in your group. Keep an eye on the clock, and continue stories after the study is over for those who can hang around and talk.

Question 10. John Stott illuminates this passage:

Paul to Agrippa (boldly confronting the king, of whom he has just been speaking to Festus in the third person): *"King Agrippa, do you believe the prophets? I know you do"* (27).

The court gasps. Has any prisoner ever before presumed to address his Royal Highness with such impertinence? Agrippa is unhorsed. Too embarrassed to give Paul a direct answer to a direct question, and too proud to allow him to dictate the topic of their dialogue, he takes evasive action with an ambiguous counter-question.

Agrippa to Paul: *"Do you think that in such a short time you can persuade me to be a Christian?"* (28).

The court gasps again. That was a clever riposte, by which the king regained the initiative. A murmur went round the audience as people discussed exactly what he meant. It was "variously represented as a trivial jest, a bitter sarcasm, a grave irony, a burst of anger, and an expression of *sincere conviction."* How would Paul respond?

Paul to Agrippa (in no doubt how he will interpret the king's words, and determined to exploit them for the gospel): *"Short time or long—I pray God that not only you but all who are listening to me today may become what I am, except for these chains"* (29).

With those words Paul lifted his hands and rattled the chains which bound him. He was sincere, the prisoner Paul. He really believed what he was talking about. He wanted everybody to be like him, including the king—everybody a Christian, but nobody a prisoner. You could not help admiring his integrity. There was also a finality about his statement, for his judges had nothing more to say. (Stott, *Message of Acts,* pp. 376-77)

STUDY 12. ACTS 27–28. PAUL IN ROME!

PURPOSE: To rejoice in Paul's reaching Rome and to have our confidence in God so affected by what he did in Paul's life that we go forth "boldly and without hindrance proclaiming the kingdom of God and teaching others about the Lord Jesus Christ" (Acts 28:31 RSV).

General note. I would urge you to lead the group in taking seriously the truth not only of these last two chapters but of the whole book of Acts. A quick summary might be appropriate. Be prepared to do such if you feel it will be helpful.

Try to help members to see the excitement of God's fulfilling his purpose. Against all odds, he has gotten Paul to Rome. Also, look at Paul's great faithfulness to God and his singleness of mind in proclaiming the gospel of Jesus Christ.

I would highly recommend a time of prayer at the end of this study.

Group discussion. Not a lot of time should be spent on this question. Be on guard so that the discussion does not get too philosophical and thus too lengthy. There are many important things to cover in this last study.

Question 1. "So far in the Acts Luke has depicted Paul as the apostle to the Gentiles, the pioneer of the three missionary expeditions, the prisoner, and the defendant. Now, however, he portrays him in a different light. He is no longer an honoured apostle, but an ordinary man among men, a lonely Christian (apart from Luke himself and Aristarchus) among nearly three hundred non-Christians, who were either soldiers or prisoners or perhaps merchants or crew. Yet Paul's God-given leadership gifts clearly emerge. 'It is quite certain,' writes William Barclay, 'that Paul was the most experienced traveler on board that ship.' Even Haenchen, who scornfully dismisses Luke's portrait of him as 'only . . . a mighty superman,' concedes that Luke fails to draw our attention adequately to Paul's expertise as a seasoned seafarer. He catalogues the apostle's eleven voyages on the Mediterranean *before* he set sail for Rome and calculates that Paul had traveled at least 3,500 miles by sea. Yet it was more than mature experience at sea which made Paul stand out as a leader on board ship; it was his steadfast Christian faith and character" (Stott, *Message of Acts,* pp. 389-90).

This is an important question. It is an overview of the passage, which is long, and focuses on its important content. Look carefully at all the ways Paul ministers to others.

Question 2. It seems to me that each time Paul ministered it was out of compassion—whether it was warning the ship leaders of loss of life and cargo (he could have just taken care of himself; 27:9-10), letting them be comforted by God's promise of safety (27:21-25) instead of keeping that to himself, encouraging them to take nourishment and stay on the ship, building them a fire in order to care for their bodies (27:31-38; 28:31), healing the islanders (28:8-9) or sharing the gospel with the Jews (28:17-20, 23-31).

Question 5. Julius trusted Paul and desired to be kind to him. Julius must have seen in Paul the character of Christ, his integrity and that he was a man worth being kind to. He trusted him. Wherever Paul was, he built relationships that honored the Lord and that communicated to people their value— even those taking him to prison and guarding him.

Question 6. "At all events, he now had complete confidence in what he was about to say. Twice he urged them to keep up their courage (22, 25). On what ground? Because none of them, he said, but only the ship, would be lost (22). How could he be so certain? Because the previous night an angel of the God to whom he belonged, and whom he served, had stood beside him (23), had told him not to be afraid, had promised that he must without fail stand trial before Caesar, and had added that God would give him (in answer to his prayers?) the lives of all his fellow passengers (24). These divine promises were the foundation of Paul's summons to everybody to maintain their courage. For he believed in God, in his character and covenant, and was convinced that he would keep his promises (25), even though the first ship would have to run aground on some island (26)" (Stott, *Message of Acts,* pp. 390-91).

Question 7. There were many ways people were affected by Paul's confidence in God. All of Paul's being was permeated with Christ. Thus, people were affected by his lifestyle, not just his preaching. Consider the broad scope of the effects of his ministry.

Question 8. Help your group to think through how people are affected by our confidence in God. What are ways that it is demonstrated?

Phyllis J. Le Peau worked with InterVarsity Christian Fellowship for over two decades in St. Louis and the Chicago metro area. She is also the author of the several Bible study guides published by Zondervan and InterVarsity Press, including the LifeGuide Bible Studies Grandparenting, Love, *and* Women of the New Testament. *She and her husband, Andy, have four married children and thirteen grandchildren.*

WHAT SHOULD
WE STUDY NEXT?

LifeGuide®
BIBLE STUDIES

Since 1985 LifeGuide® Bible Studies have provided solid inductive Bible study content with field-tested questions that get groups talking—making for a one-of-a-kind Bible study experience. This series has more than 120 titles on Old and New Testament books, character studies, and topical studies. IVP's LifeGuide Finder is a great tool for searching for your next study topic: https://ivpress.com/lifeguidefinder.

Here are some ideas to get you started.

BIBLE BOOKS

An in-depth study of a Bible book is one of the richest experiences you could have in opening up the riches of Scripture. Many groups begin with a Gospel such as Mark or John. These guides are divided into two parts so that if twenty or twenty-six weeks feels like too much to do as once, the group can feel free to do half of the studies and take a break with another topic.

A shorter letter such as Philippians or Ephesians is also a great way to start. Shorter Old Testament studies include Ruth, Esther, and Job.

TOPICAL SERIES

Here are a few ideas of short series you might put together to cover a year of curriculum on a theme.

Christian Formation: *Christian Beliefs* (12 studies by Stephen D. Eyre), *Christian Character* (12 studies by Andrea Sterk & Peter Scazzero), *Christian Disciplines* (12 studies by Andrea Sterk & Peter Scazzero), *Evangelism* (12 studies by Rebecca Pippert & Ruth Siemens).

Building Community: *Christian Community* (10 studies by Rob Suggs), *Friendship* (10 studies by Carolyn Nystrom), *Spiritual Gifts* (12 studies by Charles & Anne Hummel), *Loving Justice* (12 studies by Bob and Carol Hunter).

GUIDES FOR SPECIFIC TYPES OF GROUPS

If you have a group that is serving a particular demographic, here are some specific ideas. Also note the list of studies for seekers on the back cover.

Women's Groups: *Women of the New Testament, Women of the Old Testament, Woman of God, Women & Identity, Motherhood*

Marriage and Parenting: *Marriage, Parenting, Grandparenting*